Jump Right In
the instrumental series
Errata Sheet

Below is the correct notation for number 5, "Row, Row, Row Your Boat". Please cut out the notation for your instrument out and tape it over what is currently on the page. We are sorry for any inconvenience.

5 ROW, ROW, ROW YOUR BOAT

Flute and Oboe

Bassoon

Alto Saxophone

OBOE
SOLO BOOK 1A
REVISED EDITION

Jump Right In
the instrumental series

Richard F. Grunow
Professor of Music Education
Eastman School of Music
of the University of Rochester

Edwin E. Gordon

Christopher D. Azzara
Associate Professor of Music Education
Eastman School of Music
of the University of Rochester

AN INSTRUMENTAL METHOD DESIGNED FOR DEVELOPING AUDIATION SKILLS AND EXECUTIVE SKILLS

INSTRUMENT	BK 1	CD 1	BK1 & CD	BK 2	CD 2	BK2 & CD	SOLO BK 1A	SOLO BK 1B	SOLO BK 2	SOLO BK 3
Flute	J250	J251	J252	J289		J290	J339	J353	J150	J204
Clarinet	J253	J254	J255	J291		J292	J340	J354	J151	J205
Oboe	J256	J257	J258	J293		J294	J341	J355	J152	J206
Bassoon	J259	J260	J261	J295		J296	J342	J356	J153	J207
Alto Sax	J262	J263	J264	J297		J298	J343	J357	J154	J208
Tenor Sax	J265	J266	J267	J299		J300	J344	J358	J155	J209
Trumpet	J268	J269	J270	J301	J316	J302	J345	J359	J156	J210
Horn in F	J271	J272	J273	J303		J304	J346	J360	J157	J211
Trombone	J274	J275	J276	J305		J306	J347	J361	J158	J212
Baritone BC	J277	J278	J279	J307		J308	J348	J362	J159	J213
Baritone TC	J280	J281	J282	J309		J310	J349	J363	J160	J214
Tuba	J283	J284	J285	J311		J312	J350	J364	J161	J215
Percussion	J286	J287	J288	J313		J314	J351	J365	J162	J216
Recorder	J231	J232	J233	J247	J245CD	J245	J94		J149	J217

Revised Teacher Guide for Band Books 1 and 2 ....J315
Solo Book 1–Writing (all instruments) J167
Solo Book 2–Writing (all instruments) J168
Solo Book 3–Writing (all instruments) J203
Composition Book 1 (all instruments) J249
Revised Teacher's Guide for Recorder J235
GIA Heavy Duty Soprano Recorder M447
JRI for Strings (specify instrument)

CONCERT SELECTIONS
Full score (all twelve works) J178
Flute (J179) • Oboe (J180) • Clarinet I (J181) • Clarinet II (J182) • Bass Clarinet (J183) • Bassoon (J184) • Alto Saxophone (J185) • Tenor Saxophone (J186) • Baritone Saxophone (J187) • Trumpet I (J188) • Trumpet II (J189) • Horn (J190) • Trombone I (J191) • Trombone II (J192) • Baritone B.C. (J193) • Baritone T.C. (J194) • Tuba (J195) • Bells/Xylophone/Piano (J196) • Percussion (J197)
Demonstration compact disc J198CD

RECORDED SOLOS WITH ACCOMPANIMENTS

CD/Bk 1A:	Cassette Bk 2:	Cassette Bk 3:
J352	J148	J200
CD/Bk 1B:	CD Bk 2:	CD Bk 3:
J366	J148CD	J200CD

LISTENING

Simple Gifts	*Don Gato*	*You Are My Sunshine*
Cassette:	Cassette:	Cassette:
J229CS	J201CS	J199CS
CD:	CD:	CD:
J229CD	J201CD	J199CD

GIA Publications, Inc., 7404 S. Mason Ave., Chicago, IL 60638

NOTE TO STUDENTS, PARENTS, AND TEACHERS[1]

You may begin using *Solo Book 1A with CD* and also *Solo Book 1B with CD* from *Jump Right In: The Instrumental Series – for Winds and Percussion* when you have learned to audiate and perform many of the songs in *Student Book One*. Exemplary performances and accompaniments for the songs in this book are recorded on the CD included inside the front cover.

Try to perform the songs in this book by ear before performing them from notation. First you should listen to the songs and audiate as they are performed by the professional musician on the CD that accompanies this book. Next, you should sing the songs and learn to perform them by ear on your instrument (A and B listed below – under MUSICAL ENRICHMENT ACTIVITIES).

Notice in the notation that dynamic markings, tempo markings, stylistic markings, and articulations are not indicated. After listening to the professional musician, indicate by marking with a pencil the dynamics, tempos, stylistic markings, and articulation for each solo in the manner that it is performed on the CD. The *Music Theory* section of *Student Book Two* and *Composition Book One* provide information to help mark your music. Mark the notation with a pencil because you may decide to try musical ideas that are different from those used by the professional musician on the recording. Ask your instrumental music teacher for suggestions.

Additional MUSICAL ENRICHMENT ACTIVITIES are listed below for each song. The *Fingering Chart, Slide Position Chart,* or *Keyboard Organization Chart* in the back of this book will help you when locating unfamiliar pitches on your instrument.

You will enjoy performing all the songs in this book with your friends. When performing a few songs, however, you may wish to perform the melody an octave above or below the written melody. In some cases you may wish to perform the melody in a different keyality (start on a different note). At times, you may enjoy just listening to the performances on the CD.

Chord symbols (C, G7, Dm, etc.) are included above the music notation. You may use the chord symbols when learning to perform accompaniments, variations, and improvisations of the songs. Your instrumental music teacher will explain how to use chord symbols.

MUSICAL ENRICHMENT ACTIVITIES

   A. Sing the song. You may sing the song in a different keyality (start on a different note) than found on the CD.
   B. Perform the song on your instrument by ear in the same tonality and keyality that is on the CD.
   C. Perform the song in a second keyality.
   D. Perform the song in a third keyality.
   E. Perform the song with a friend who plays the same or a different instrument.
   F. Perform the song in a different meter. (For example, play duple meter tunes in triple meter and play triple meter tunes in duple meter.)
   G. Perform the song in a different tonality. (For example, play major tonality songs in minor tonality, and play minor tonality songs in major tonality.)
   H. Perform the bass line for the song.
   I. Perform an improvisation or harmony part for the song.
   J. Indicate the notation for the song. Ask your instrumental music teacher about *Solo Books – Writing*.

A☐	C☐	E☐	G☐	I☐
B☐	D☐	F☐	H☐	J☐

---

[1] *Solo Book 1A with CD* (50 tunes) *and Solo Book 1B with CD* (50 tunes) from *Jump Right In: The Instrumental Series* were originally released as *Solo Book One* (100 tunes). Solo Books 1A and 1B feature a varied musical repertoire that follows the key sequence of instruction in *Jump Right In: The Instrumental Series – for Winds and Percussion.*

4

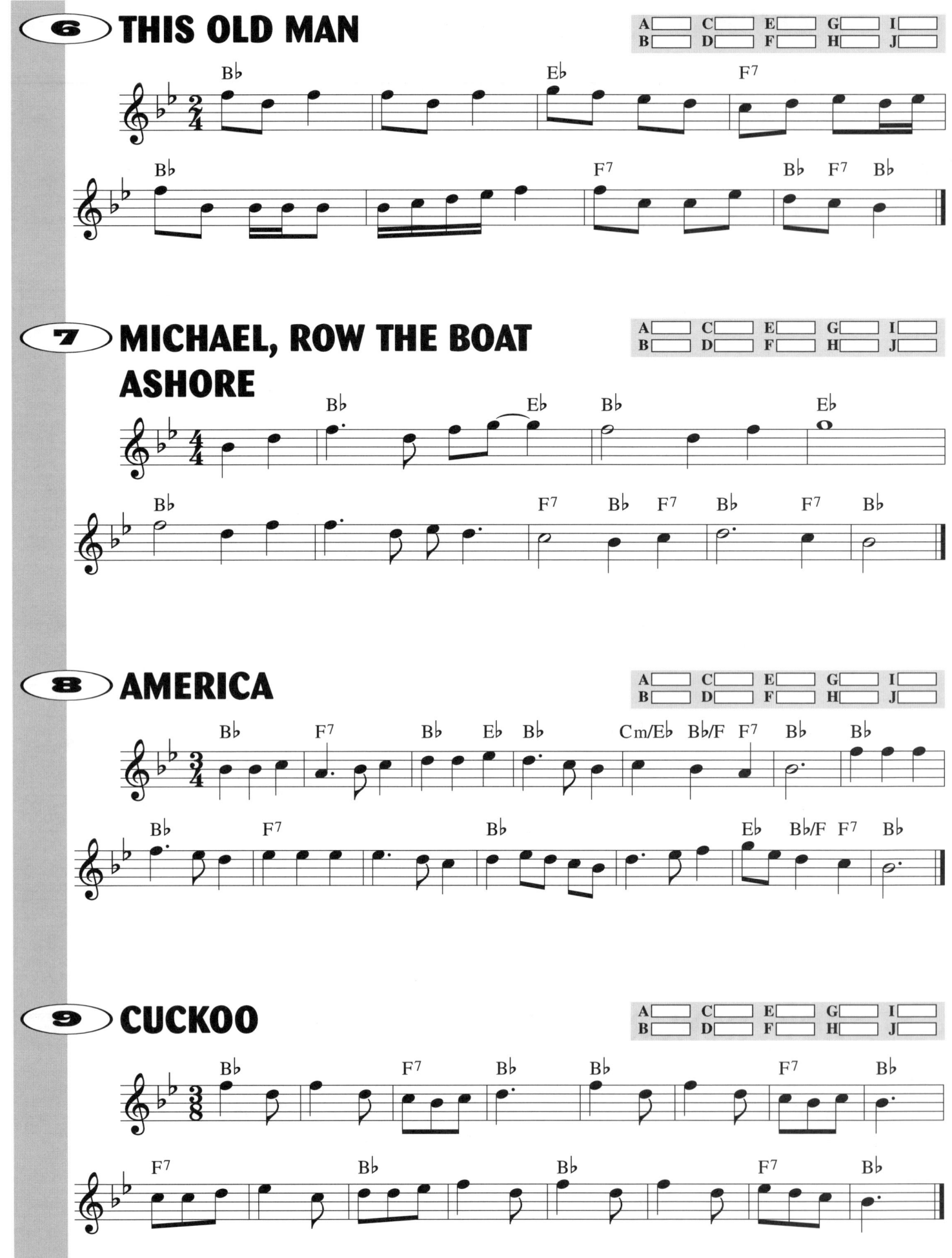

14 ACH DU LEIBER AUGUSTINE

A		C		E		G		I	
B		D		F		H		J	

15 LITTLE BROWN JUG

A		C		E		G		I	
B		D		F		H		J	

16 NOW THE DAY IS OVER

A		C		E		G		I	
B		D		F		H		J	

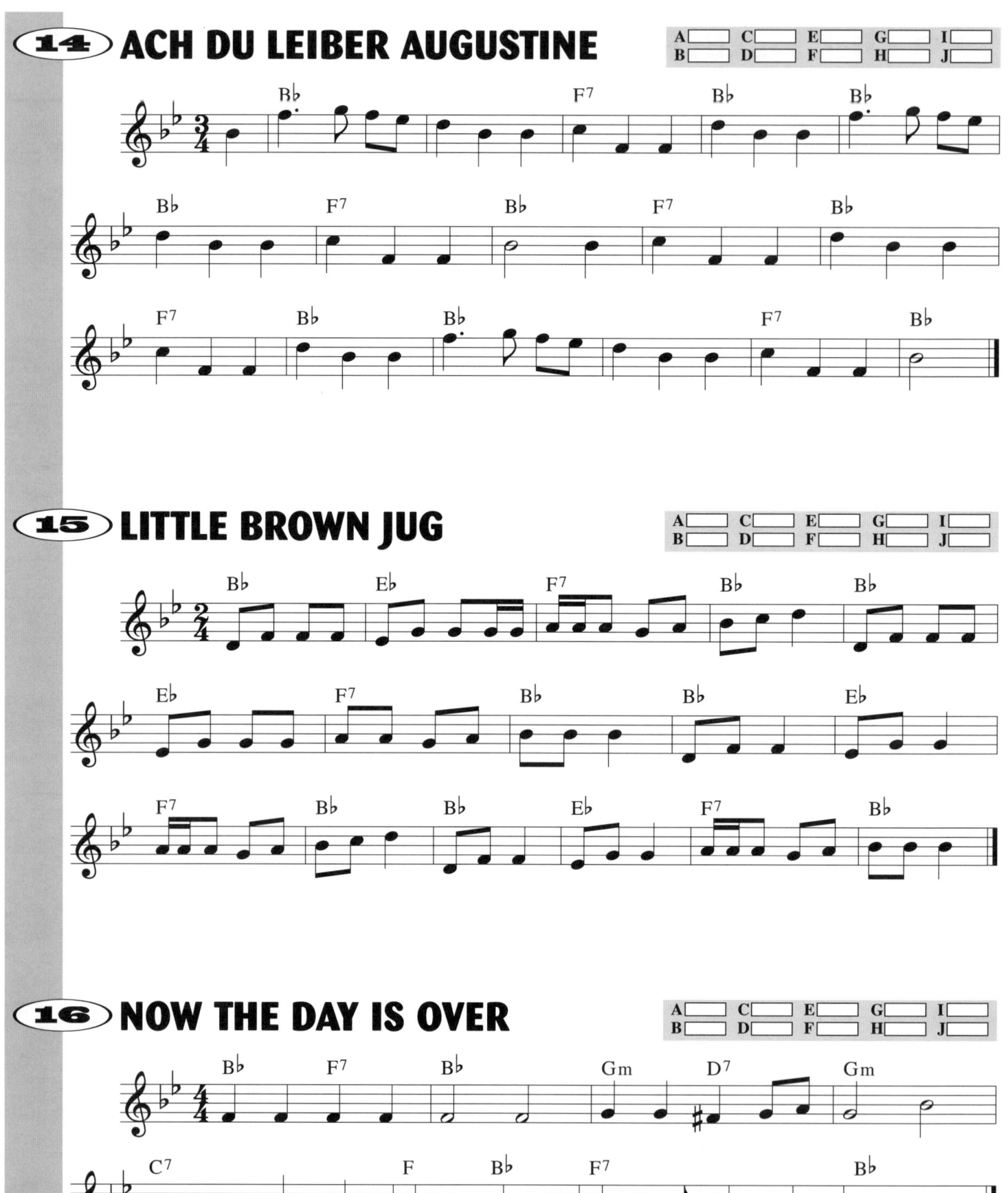

17 THREE BLIND MICE

A		C		E		G		I	
B		D		F		H		J	

18 RIG A JIG JIG

A		C		E		G		I	
B		D		F		H		J	

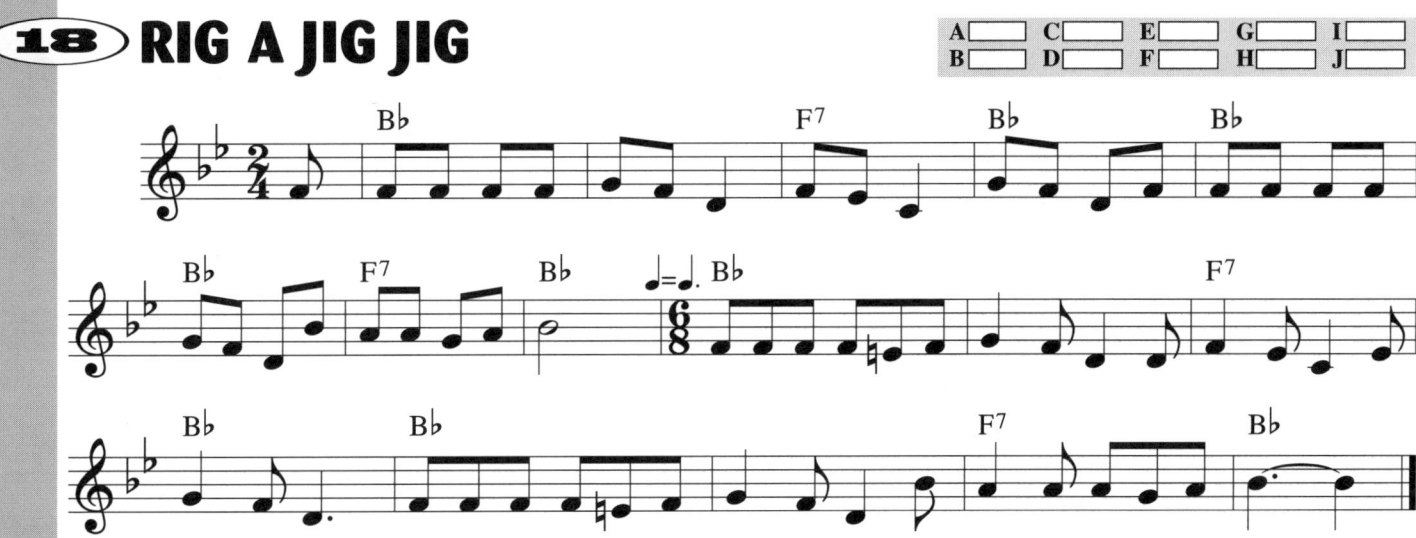

19 POP, GOES THE WEASEL

A		C		E		G		I	
B		D		F		H		J	

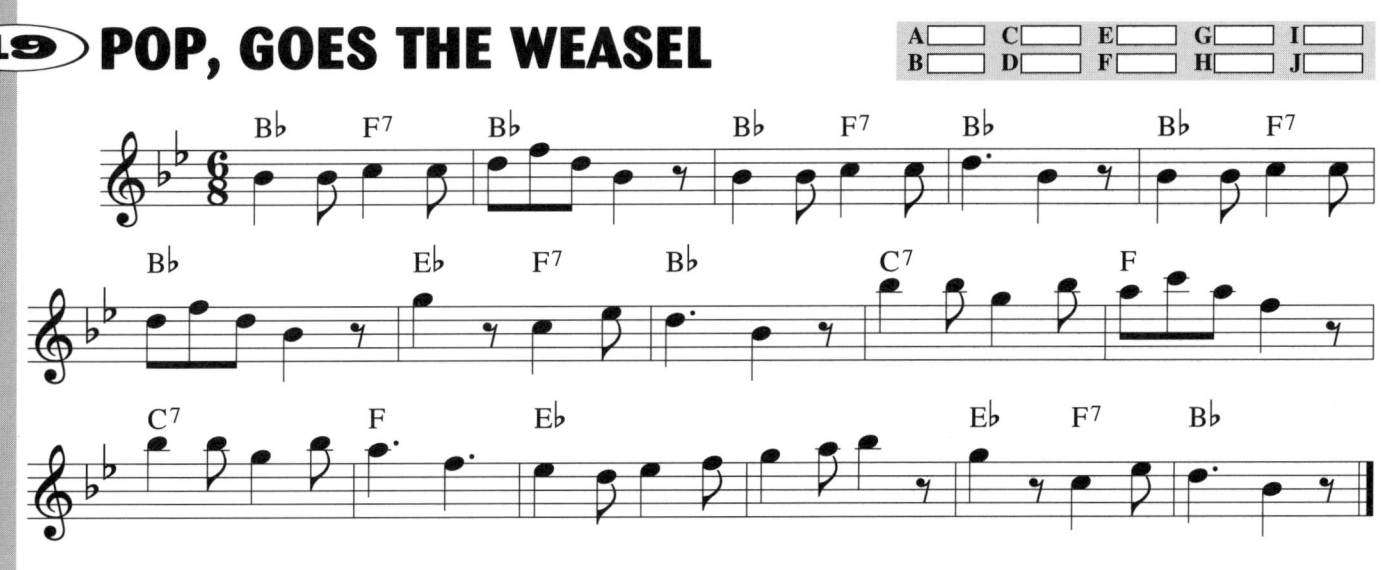

28 ALMA MATER

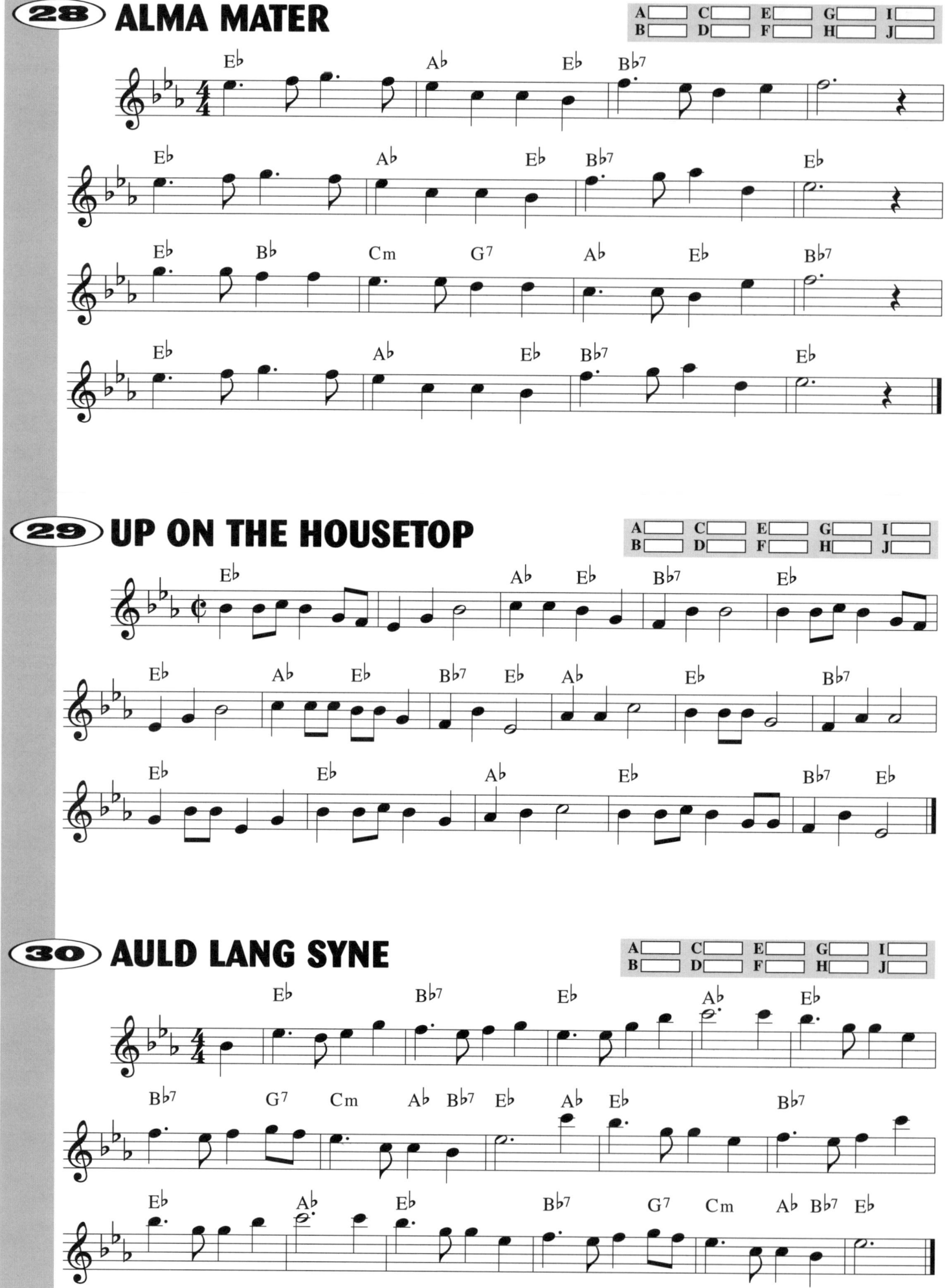

29 UP ON THE HOUSETOP

30 AULD LANG SYNE

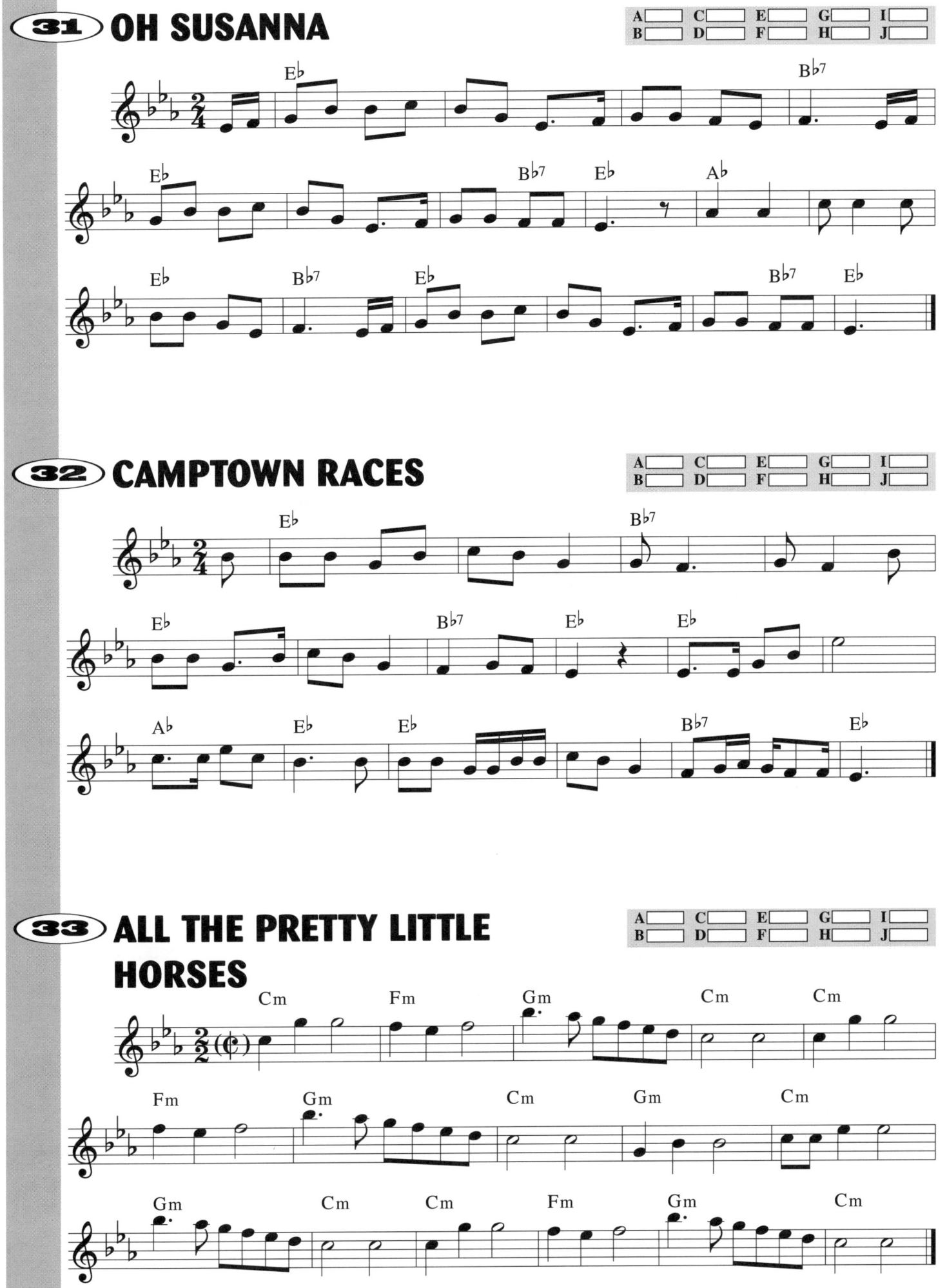

12

38 MEXICAN HAT DANCE

A		C		E		G		I	
B		D		F		H		J	

39 BLOW THE MAN DOWN

A		C		E		G		I	
B		D		F		H		J	

40 JINGLE BELLS

A		C		E		G		I	
B		D		F		H		J	

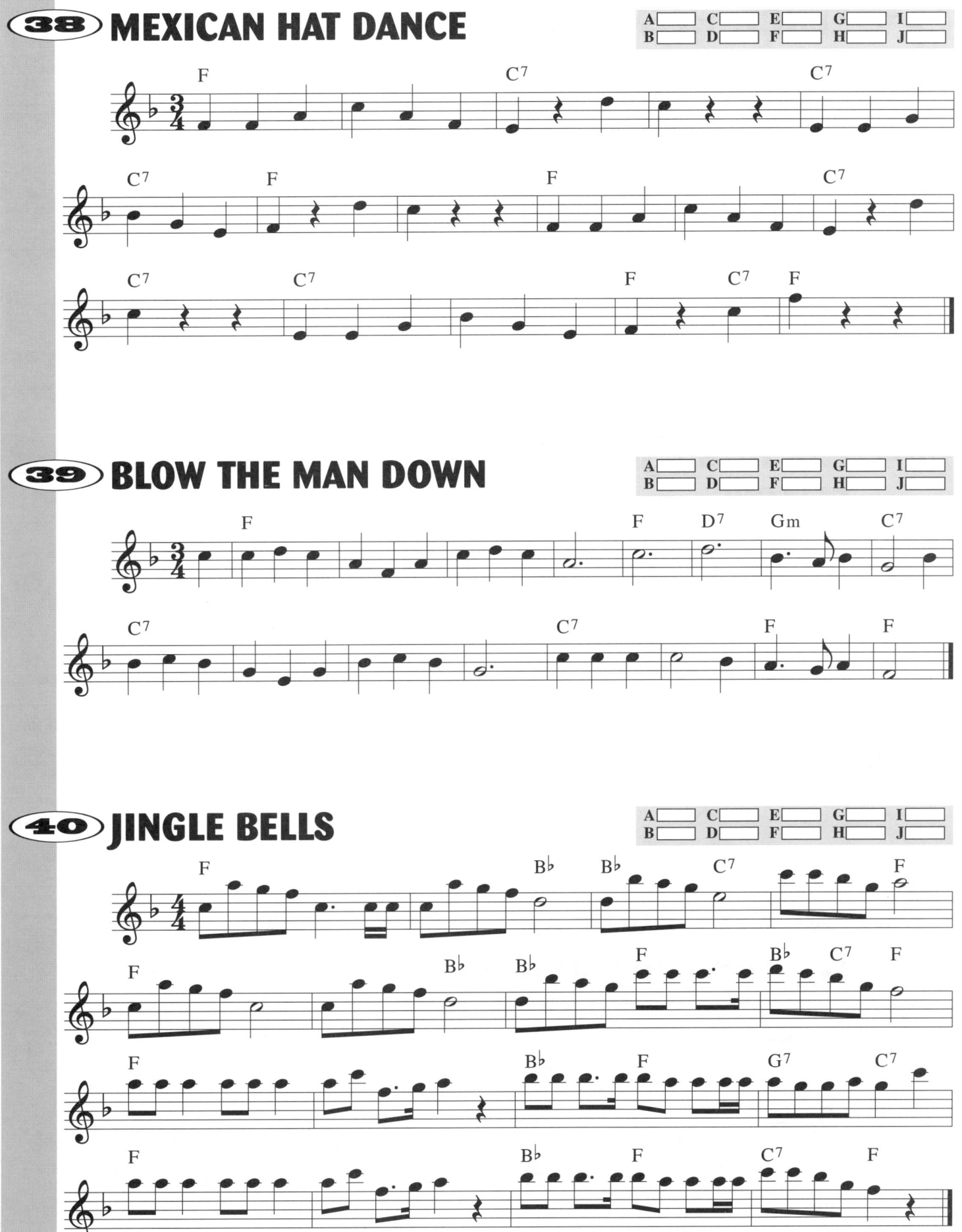

14

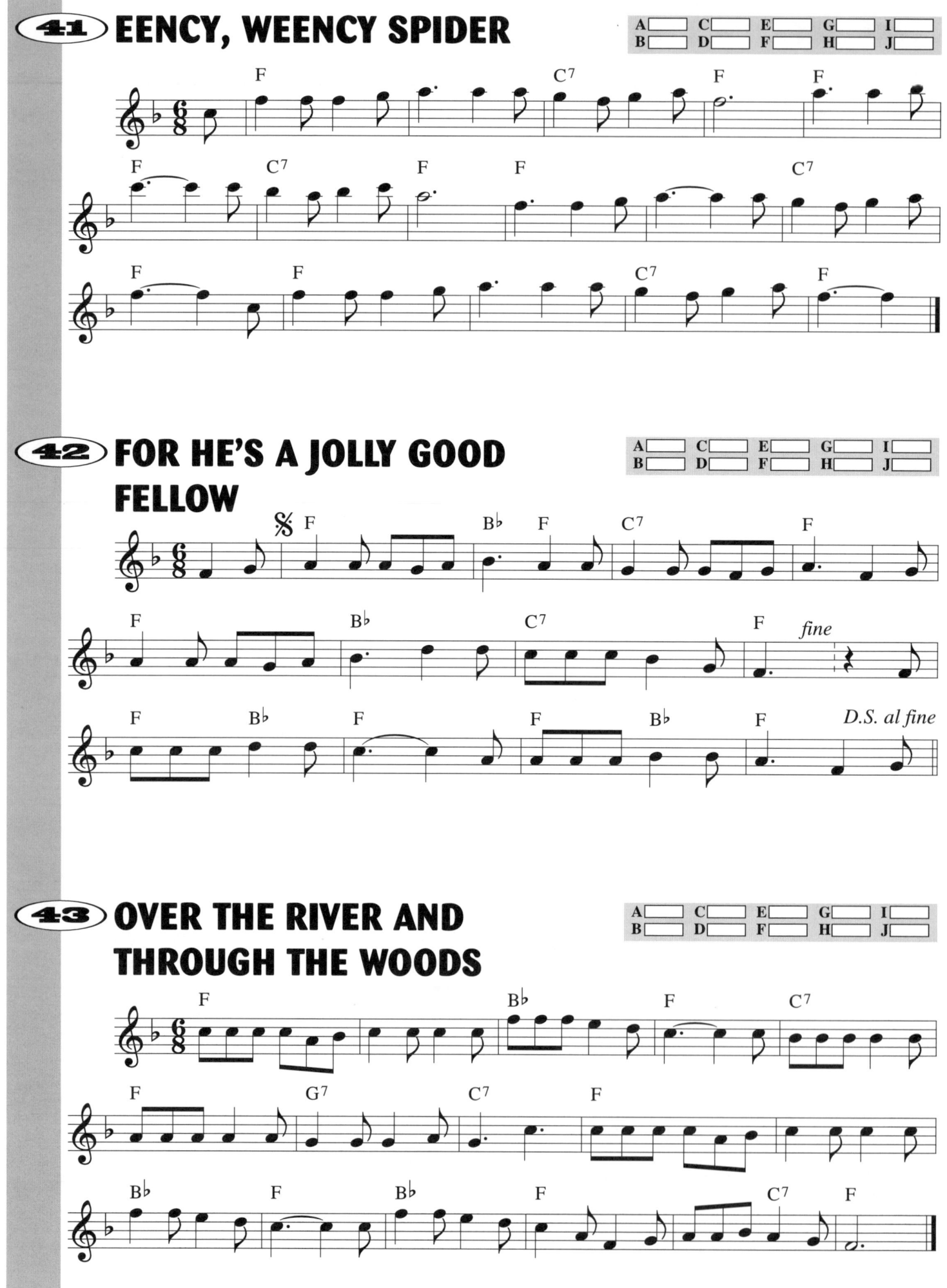

16